TSUYOSHI WATANABE
DRAGONS RIOTING

男獄爆

DRAGONS RIOTING
04

04
TSUYOSHI WATANABE

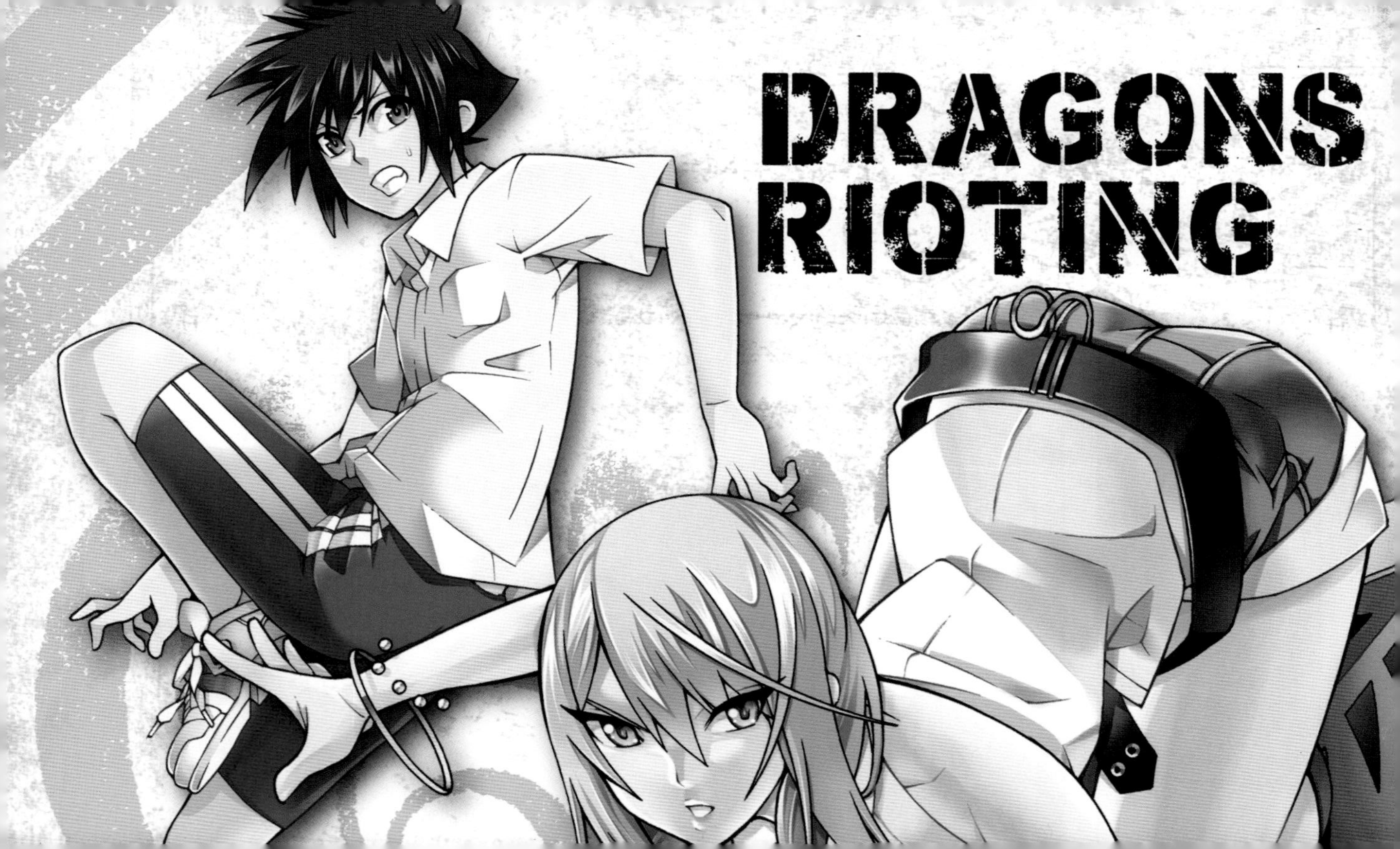
DRAGONS
RIOTING

MIIIN
(BZZZZ)
PURU
(JIGGLE)
MUCHI
(TIGHT)
NOTHING BEATS THE POOL IN THE SUMMER.
KEIKO, THERE'S NO EATING DURING CLASS!!
41°C IS THE MOST SUITABLE TEMPER-ATURE.
THAT'S FOR A BATH, MAKOTO!!
DRAGON 15
CHANCE ENCOUNTER

DAD... AT LONG LAST...
LA LA!
LA-LA-LA-LA-LA-LA!
...THE MOST LOATH-SOME OF ALL SEASONS HAS ARRIVED.
SUMMER —
"WHEN MY MISSION IS OVER, I'M GOING TO PROPOSE." IS ONE WAY TO PUT IT.
AND IN MY HEART—
...A DEATH FLAG...
...STANDS STRAIGHT AND STRONG (ABOVE ME).

IN THAT CASE...
CLEAR MY MIND.
SU (BREATHE)
KEEP IT UNDISTURBED.
WAY OF THE WOLF'S FANG—
HAH!
BYUOOOO (WHOOSH)
PIKIIIIN (SHIIIING)
T-TEACHER!! THE POOL WATER...
...SUDDENLY FROZE OVER!
WHAT THE—!?
WE'LL HAVE TO CANCEL SWIM CLASS THEN!
AWWWWWW!
OF COURSE, I'M NOT ACTUALLY CAPABLE OF MAGIC LIKE THAT...
NEXT ARE THE BOYS.
DO FIVE 25-METER LAPS IN THE FRONT CRAWL!!
PI (FWEET)
CHAPU (SPLISH)

YAY! HEE HEE!
HEH HEH!
GUH...
I'M GONNA GET KNOCKED OUT ON THE SURFACE ...
ZABO (SPLOOSH)
...BUT UNDER WATER...
!?
PURIRIN (JIGGLE)
...THE BOTTOM IS FULL OF BOTTOMS !?
GOBOBO (BLORP)

ZABAAAA (SPLORSH)
GIRLS OF SUMMER—
HE'S SO TENSE.
SHAME-FUL.
MY LIFE IS IN PERIL!!
THIS IS THE ANSWER TO MY PROBLEM...
CHIIIIN (FREEZE)
!!
YURA (FLOAT)
HE'S DOING THE SAME THING I AM...?
KOPO (BLOOP)
コポポ
PO

!?
GOBOBO (BLORP)
WH-WHAT'S THIS HOLE...?
GOBOBOBO
ONE OF THE SEVEN WONDERS OF NANGOKUREN IS THE "THERMAE HOLE."
IT'S A HOLE THAT APPEARS RANDOMLY AND WITHOUT WARNING IN THE POOL...
IT'S AWFUL.
HOW SCARY!
...AND IF YOU GET SUCKED INTO IT, YOU'LL BE TRANSPORTED TO AN ANCIENT ROMAN BATH.
HA-HA-HA... NO WAY.
IT IIIIIIIS!
BA
BA (FLAIL)
!!
GOBO
!?
GOBO
GOBO
GA (GRAB)

PAAAAN (SPLOOOSH)
THE SCHOOL OF THE BLUE MOON RE-FLECTED ON A LAKE
WAY OF THE ROARING FISH—HORI-ZONTAL ORCA
EEK!
WHAT THE!?
A FART!?
AN ERUP-TION!?
SUTA (TMP)
KOFF!
KOFF!
TH-THAT WAS CLOSE......
WE ALMOST ENDED UP IN ROME...
OH... YOU OKAY?
PEKO (BOW)
Y-YES, I'M FINE.
I'M SO SORRY ABOUT THAT.
UH... YOU'RE...
SINCE THERE ARE SO FEW GUYS, CLASS WAS COED......

MY NAME IS MAROKICHI.
OH... MAROKICHI-KUN...
I'M RINTARO.
V-VERY NICE TO MEET YOU.
SORRY AGAIN.
PEKO
PEKO
UH... LIKEWISE.
SO, UM...
WHAT WERE YOU DOING THERE ANYWAY?
OH, UH, WELL...
IT'S A LITTLE EMBARRASSING TO ADMIT, BUT...
...I'M NOT VERY GOOD WITH GIRLS.
UM...
I CAN'T REALLY GET NEAR THEM...
HUH ...?

TH-THE TRUTH IS, I'D LIKE TO BE FRIENDS WITH THEM.
BUT EVEN THOUGH I ENROLLED IN THE SCHOOL I'VE ALWAYS ASPIRED TO ATTEND...
...WITH THIS MANY GIRLS AROUND...
...I'VE ACTUALLY GROWN EVEN MORE AFRAID OF THEM...
I KNOW... IT'S PRETTY PATHETIC.
!?
GASHI (GRAB)

I GET YOU. I TOTALLY GET YOU!
BUN (SHAKE)
BUN
R-RINTARO-SAN, ARE YOU ALSO UNEASY AROUND GIRLS?
FOR PERSONAL REASONS...
...VERY MUCH SO.
I... I SEE...
THIS IS THE FIRST TIME I'VE EVER MET A KINDRED SPIRIT.
KINDRED SPIRIT...
I LIKE THE SOUND OF THAT.
KUU (SWOON)
I'VE FOUND A COMRADE.
AND HE'S ACTUALLY NORMAL FOR ONCE.
BIII (BEEEEP)
AH...!
SA (SWISH)
?

S-SORRY.
I'D BETTER HEAD BACK.
SU (SWF)
OH... RIGHT.
IT'S STILL CLASS AFTER ALL.
I'LL GO WITH YOU.
UH... ACTUALLY ...I'M SORRY.
I THINK I'M JUST GOING TO GO HOME EARLY FOR THE DAY.
UH... WH-WHY?
YOU OKAY?
G-GOODBYE!
TA
TA (TMP)
UH...
?
TH...THEN I HOPE WE CAN TALK MORE NEXT TIME...
...MARO-KICHI-KUN!!

YES!
KII (CREAK)
KIIIN (DOOONG)
KOOON (DONG)
KAAAN (DING)
OH... OOPS!
CLASS IS OVER.
BA (HOP)
TA (TMP)
TA
TA
Boys' Locker Room
I KNOW IT WAS YOU GOONS!
!!

I CAN'T THINK OF ANYBODY ELSE IT COULD BE!!
ACCEPT YOUR FATE.
YOU'VE GOT IT ALL WRONG!
WE DIDN'T DO NOTHING!
H-HOLD ON. WHAT'S GOING ON HERE!?
TA
TA (TMP)
RINTARO! HELP!!
SAVE US, BRO!!
AYANE'S UNDERGARMENTS WERE STOLEN.
AND THESE TWO ARE THE CULPRITS.
WH-WHAT'D YOU DO THAT FOR!?
HURRY UP AND GIVE THEM BACK!!
HEY!
DON'T YOU TREAT US LIKE CRIMINALS TOO!
YOU SCUMBAG!!

A PUNCH OR TWO SHOULD HAVE THEM FESSING UP.
PAKI (POP)
PAKI
STOP IT! I'M AGAINST VIOLENCE!!
SA (CLING)
SA
...
O GREAT GANDHI, SAVE US!
PLEASE, RINTARO.
WE HONESTLY DIDN'T DO IT.
PLEASE BELIEVE US.
THE ONLY ONE WHO'LL BELIEVE US IN THIS WHOLE SCHOOL...
...IS YOU.
KO-SUKE-KUN...
TA-MAO-KUN...
FINE. I GOT IT.
HUH?

I WILL FIND THE TRUE CULPRIT.
KA (FLASH)
MASTER...
HUH? YOU?
YES!
I DON'T LIKE BEING ATTACKED FOR SOMETHING I DIDN'T DO.
YEAH. I'M A MASOCHIST, BUT THIS IS TOO MUCH.
BOSO (PSST)
BUT, MASTER...
...ARE YOU CAPABLE OF THAT KIND OF GUMSHOE WORK?
Locker Room
JUST LEAVE IT TO ME.
KACHA (KLATCH)
AFTER ALL—
BA (WHIP)
I OWN THE ENTIRE DVD BOX SET...
...OF FURUHATA NINZABURO.
TEDEEEEN (TA-DAA)
RIN TARO
TA CHI BA NA
IT'S JUST LIKE FURUHATA TO NOT WEAR A TIE

きょとん
KYOTON (STUNNED)
MAS-TER?
THERE'S ALSO MULTIPLE PERSONALITY DETECTIVE PSYCHO, KINDAICHI AND CONAN...
I'VE READ THEM ALL.
HE SURE IS COCKY FOR HAVING ONLY READ THAT STUFF...
IT'S QUITE PAINFUL TO WIT-NESS.
NOW THEN...FIRST THINGS FIRST. INVESTIGATING THE SCENE OF THE CRIME.
HMMM... WE HAVE A PHRASE CALLED "GOING OVER THE SCENE OF THE CRIME A HUNDRED TIMES."
HANMAA KANMAA.
THAT'S JUST WHAT A CELEBRITY IM-PERSONATING HIM SAYS.
THAT'S HOLLYWOOD ZAKOSHI-SHOU.
AYANE-SAN.
LET'S HEAD TO THE SCENE OF THE CRIME.
HEH-HEH-HEH.
O-OKAY...
RINTARO, GOOD LUCK.
LET'S GET OUT OF HERE.
くる
KURU (TURN)
YOU GUYS AREN'T OFF THE HOOK YET.
Y-YOU'RE TYING US UP!?
HAAH! HAAH!
I DON'T MIND IT.

THIS IS WHERE IT HAPPENED.
Girls' Locker Room
THERE'S NOBODY INSIDE RIGHT NOW, SO YOU CAN GO ON IN.
I DO NOT...
...WANT TO GO IN THERE.
I'LL HAVE TO DECLINE.
L-LET'S SWEEP AROUND THE AREA FIRST.
KURU (TURN)
HUH...? BUT THIS IS THE ONLY WAY IN.
WAI WAI (GAB)
URK ...!?
WH-WH... WHAT THE? I'M TRAPPED ...
UH... COULD YOU WAIT A MOMENT?

DO I ENTER THE LION'S DEN...
Girls' Locker
チラ
CHIRA (GLANCE)
...OR GET MAULED BY A PACK OF LIONS THEMSELVES ...?
HEE HEE!
HEH HEH HEH.
THE LION'S DEN IT IS...!!
AT LEAST THERE'S NOBODY THERE.
BA (DART)
GACHA (KLATCH)
!?
ふわっ
FUWA (WAFT)
GHH...
CHOCOLATE DISCO ♪
SA (SWISH)
...THE PLACE IS PERFUMED WITH THE SCENT OF GIRLS.
EVEN WITH NOBODY HERE...

THE SCHOOL...
CLEAR MY MIND.
KEEP IT UNDISTURBED.
...OF THE BLUE MOON REFLECTED ON A LAKE
KOKI (CRACK)
KI
WAY OF THE BALLED-UP MOUSE—
TELEPATHY
TAN (THUD)
BIRI (SHUDDER)
BIRI
BIRI
BIRI
BIRI
BIRI
BA
BA (SLAM)
BA
BA

PWAH!
BA (LUNGE)
PHEW...
HM?
MUD?
TH-THIS IS...!!
SU (STEP)
!?
C-COULD THAT BE THE THIEF!?
IF I FOLLOW HIM, I CAN CATCH HIM.
SUTA (TMP)

EXCUSE ME!
DA (DASH)
PLEASE WAIT!
DA
!!
CHIRA (GLANCE)
TO (TAP)
!!
ZASHA (SWOOSH)
HE'S GET-TING AWAY...
NO MIS-TAKE ABOUT IT!
GU (DIG)

GYUN
(ZOOM)
!!
BA
(LUNGE)
ZA
(ZSH)
ZA
ZA
ZA
ZA
ZA

Zuuuuun (THOOOM)
Plaque: Principal Statue
KA (CLACK)
!?
CHA (CHK)
ZAN (SLICE)

!?
THE SCHOOL ...
CLEAR MY MIND.
SU (BREATHE)
KEEP IT UNDIS-TURBED.
...OF THE BLUE MOON REFLECTED ON A LAKE
KURU (TURN)
KURU
GURUN (SPIN)
GURUN

WAY OF THE SNAKE BONE
GYURU (SPIN)
RU
RU

GAGO (CRASH)
HYU (ZIP)
TA (TAK)
ZA (ZSH)
ZA
ZA
SHUUUUU (SSSSSHH)
...
GARA (RMBL)
PARA
PARA (CRMBL)
GARA
HY-PER-BOLIC ARM STAB

THAT'S FAR ENOUGH.
!?
チラ
CHIRA (GLANCE)
IS THAT A WORM TECH-NIQUE...?
IT'S A SNAKE.

WAIT... A GIRL!?
DID YOU STEAL AYANE-SAN'S UNDERWEAR?
CHA (CHK)
KIRE (CUT)
BAN (BADUM)
WH- WHAT'RE YOU DOIIIIIIING!?
BA (BLOCK)
BA
WH- WHY'S SHE SUDDENLY CHANGING!?
KIGA
KIGA (STRIP)
SHE MUST BE AN ERORIST !!

OH...!
REN
...OLDER SISTER.
WHENEVER HER CLOTHES WERE EVEN THE LEAST BIT DAMAGED ...
...SHE'D CHANGE NO MATTER WHERE WE WERE.
SHE CARRIED AROUND SEVERAL BACKUP OUTFITS WITH HER.
TEEE TE TE (RING)
TEEE TE TE
!!
PI (BEEP)
HELLO?
BIKU (JUMP)
RIN-CHAN, LONG TIME NO HEAR!
EEP!?
How've you been doing?
Is Kito good too?
PYOKO (YOINK)
UH... AH...
THAT VOICE—

MELL-SAN!?
NEE HEE HEE.
ACTUALLY, GET THIS—REN DECIDED TO COME SEE YOU, RIN-CHAN.
YOU'VE NEVER MET HER BEFORE, RIGHT?
So I thought I'd describe her for you.
CHIRA (GLANCE)
D-DON'T TELL ME, THIS PERSON IS...
KYU (TUG)

THE DRAGON OF SEVERE WAVES—REN
GOKU (GULP)
S-STOP STARING AT ME LIKE THAT...
SA (SWISH)
SA
OH...
S-SORRY.

SO YOU'RE...
...RINTARO TACHIBANA.
......
YEAH...
SFX: PYON (HOP)
!!
KITO, LONG TIME NO SEE.
SUTO (TMP)
(^o^)
DRAGON·16
CONCEALE
VOICE
SO HE'S STAYING WITH YOU NOW, IS HE?
I HEARD IT FROM MELL.
I-I SEE.
WHY'S SHE SPEAKING WITH HER BACK TO ME?

But she's pretty shy around guys...

...so she can't even look them in the eye!!

She's really a disappointment of a girl.

Put her on!!
U-UM... IT'S FROM MELL-SAN.
ス::
SU (PASS)
IS THIS A BATON?
!!
WHAT IS IT...
...MELL?
HAAAAAAAH!
ピク
PIKU (TWITCH)

NOT EVEN RIN-CHAN'S GOOD ENOUGH?
What do you mean by not good enough?
I'M NOT AS SHY OF GUYS...
...AS YOU THINK I AM!!
SINCE RIN-CHAN'S NOT LIKE OTHER GUYS...
...I THOUGHT FOR SURE YOU'D BE OKAY WITH HIM.
Hey, listen to what people are telling you.
NOPEEE (SPLAT)
Oh, well. I'll be there soon.
Don't be too hard on Rin—
BUCHI (CLICK)
SHE HUNG UP ON HER!
HM...
......
SA (SWISH)

UM, SO...
WHY DID YOU RUN AWAY FROM ME BEFORE?
SU (SWF)
......
I WAS ONLY CHASING YOU BECAUSE YOU KEPT RUNNING...
A-ABOUT THAT.
KURU (TURN)
GASHI (GRAB)
BIRI (RIP)
I-IF A GUY TELLS ME TO "WAIT"...
...O-O-OF COURSE I'M GOING TO THINK HE'S TRYING TO PICK ME UP!
MOJI
MOJI (SQUIRM)
MOJI
TH-TH-THAT'S WHAT YOU CALL HITTING ON GIRLS.
AND I JUST DON'T L-LIKE THAT KIND OF RUDE BEHAVIOR!!
R-RIGHT. I GUESS YOU'VE GOT A POINT...
THERE'S NO WAY A GIRL WOULD STEAL OTHER GIRLS' PANTIES.
LABEL: JUMPED TO CONCLUSIONS
MM...
m(_ _)m
PEKO
PEKO (BOW)

ぬぎっ
NUGI (STRIP)
DON'T WORRY, KITO. I'LL FIX IT RIGHT UP.
EEP!! SHE'S DOING IT AGAIN!
CLEAR MY MIND.
EEP IT NDIS- RBED.
TAN (TAK)
THE SCHOOL...
...OF THE BLUE MOON REFLECTED ON A LAKE
GAGO (CRUNCH)

KA (CLACK)
KA
KA
!?
BUO (WHOOSH)
WAY OF THE SLEEPING SHEEP —
PLEASE ...
...TAKE YOUR TIME.
FIT-TING ROOM
WHAT'S THIS AL ABOUT?
BECAUSE YOU'RE GOING TO BE ENGAGING IN ERORIST ACTIONS...
I KNEW SHE WAS AN ERO-RIST.
NOW, WHILE I STILL HAVE A CHANCE.
DA (DASH)
AND WITH THAT, GOOD-BYE!
CHA (CHK)

KURUN (SPIN)
KURUN
DOGGAAA (BLAAAST)
HUH?
BA (FWIP)
BA
BA

KA (CLACK)
KA
KA
KA
KA
!!
REN (-SAN)...
...RETURNED THE BRICKS TO WHERE THEY CAME FROM!?
PISHIIIN (SHIIIING)
WHEN IT COMES TO TETRIS I'M PRETTY GOOD TOO.
NUU (LOOM)
EEP!!
MIIIIN (BZZZZ)
MIN
MIN

UM, SO...
ARE YOU SURE YOU SHOULDN'T BE AT COLLEGE?
......
JIIII (STARE)
......
CHIRA (GLANCE)
SA (SWISH)
......
JIIII
H-HEY... ISN'T THAT ...?
ZAWA
ZAWA (MURMUR)
UH... YEAH! IT IS!
N-NO WAY...!!
ZAWA
ZAWA (CHATTER)
BUT WHY !?

REN-SENPAI!!
EEEEK! REN-SAAAN!
ZUDA (CROWD)
IT'S BEEN SO LONG!
!?
EE-EEE-AAA-AAH!
I'M COMPLETELY DEFEATED BY YOUR STARES!?
REN-CHAAAN!
TA
TA
TA (TMP)
!!
GA (TRIP)
WAH!

ぽす
POSU (POOMF)
むにん
MUNIN (MOOSH)
GRK!
IT'S BEEN TOO LONG!
MISA... YOU HAVEN'T CHANGED AT ALL.
HUH, WELL IF IT ISN'T REN-SENPAI.
WHAT'RE YOU DOING HERE?
SHAKIIIN (FREEEEZE)
CHI-YOKO, KAKO...
...ARE YOU STILL TRAIN-ING?
LONG TIME NO SEE.
I THOUGHT I SMELLED SOMETHING TASTY.
KA (CLACK)

ZA (ZSH)
SO IT'S YOU...
...REN.
KYOKA...
OOOH!!
SO THE STRONGEST DRAGON AND LEGENDARY DRAGON ARE SIDE BY SIDE.
ZAWA (CHATTER)
REN-SENPAI'S AURA IS THE REAL DEAL, AS USUAL.
ZAWA
KYOKA-CHAN WON'T LOSE EITHER.
ZAWA
LOOK AT THAT.
IT'S THE DRAGON OF SEVERE WAVES.
SHE SEEMS AWFULLY CHUMMY WITH THE THIRD-YEARS.
THOUGH SHE'S NOT VERY FAMILIAR WITH US SECOND-YEARS.

EXCEPT FOR ONE PERSON... RIGHT?
THAT PERSON NO LONGER ...
SU (STEP)
...MATTERS AT NANGOKU-REN.
GACHA (KLATCH)
KA (CLIK) KA
SU (STEP)

JI (STARE)
WHY DID YOU COME BY TODAY?
JUST SOME PRIVATE BUSI-NESS.
CHIRA (GLANCE)
!!
EEEK! SHE'S LOOKING THIS WAY!
OUR EYES MET!
KYORO (TURN)
KYORO
WHAT'S UP?
......

HMMM...
WE SAID WE'D FIND THE PANTIES THIEF OURSELVES, BUT...
とぼ
TOBO (PLOD)
とぼ
TOBO
...MAKOTO'S GOT A MEETING WITH THE NAGINATA CLUB...
ぽす
POSU (POOMF)
...AND I'M HUNGRY ANYWAY.
MAYBE I'LL MEET UP WITH AYANE.
!?
ZOKU (CHILL)

ZUBAAAA
(ZWOOOOSH)
!!
WHOA!?
DOZUUU
(SLAAAAM)
BI
(SLICE)
KUH...
WH-
WHAT
THE!?
BA
(FWIP)

ZUUUN (LOOOM)
!!
FIRST YOU LAUNCH A SURPRISE ATTACK...
ZA (STANCE)
KOOOO (WOOOO)
...AND THEN YOU LET OFF A WICKEDLY MURDEROUS VIBE...
ZUKI (THROB)
TCH...

GUESS I'LL HAVE TO TAKE YOU ON, EH!?
!!
BO (WHOOSH)
GOGAA (CRUUUNCH)
SHUUUU (SSSHHH)

!?
GASHI (SLAM)
YOU'RE SO MASSIVE ...
GURU (FLIP)
SHOW ME WHAT YOU'VE GOT!
KEIKO TIJERA SPECIAL
DOGOO (BOOOM)

TA
(TMP)
PHEW...
ZUUUN
(THOOOM)
ZA
(ZISH)
SHEESH.
WHO IS THIS GUY ANYWAY?
PURU
(JIGGLE)
KA
(FLASH)
G-GUH...
N... NO...
BURU
(TRMBL)
BURU
ST-STOP...
BURU

BARII (RIP)
!!
TAYU (JIGGLE)
MISHI (BULGE)
MEKIKI (CREAK)
BIKI (SNAP)
!?
HE CAN STILL MOVE...!?
GABA (JUMP)
UWOOOOOOOAAH!

BON (BOOSH)
HUH!?
GYUDO (SLAM)
BYO (WHOOSH)
GUH...
GICHI
GICHI (SCRAPE)
H-HE'S FAST!

GO (BLAST)
!?
ZUKI (THROB)
GAKU (DROP)
HYU (WHOOSH)
!!
......

BO (WHOOSH)
KYORO (TURN)
キョロ
?
KYORO
キョロ
FUOO (WHOOSH)
KUH ... ...
!?
SU (PEEK)

AYANE!!
!!
YOU'LL BE OKAY HERE, KEIKO.
SU (KNEEL)
S-SOR-RY...
PASA (FWAP)
BOO...
... BIES ...
ZA (STANCE)

HUGE TIT-TIES—
IN A SCHOOL BATH-ING SUIT—
HUH ...?
I- IT'S... NO GOOD.
I...CAN'T TAKE... MUCH MORE...
GUNE (TWIST)
GUNE
I... I...
ST- STOP...!!
DA (DASH)
UWOOOOOAH!
!!
BA (HOP)
BA
BA
WHAT ON EARTH ...
...WAS THAT ...?

KEIKO!
YOU OKAY!?
TA TA (TMP)
AYANE...
HERE...
!?
I PINCHED IT...
...OFFA HIM...
HEH HEH...
NIKO (GRIN)
WE'LL TRACK HIM DOWN USING THIS...
AND NEXT TIME... FOR SURE...
...I'LL... KNOCK HIM... FLAT...
......
GU (GRIP)

PHEW... I FINALLY GOT AWAY.
TA TA TA (TMP)
BACK TO HUNTING DOWN THE CULPRIT.
NOW, THEN...
I SAID I'D GO OVER THE SCENE OF THE CRIME A HUNDRED TIMES, BUT...
...THE BEST CLUE...
...WILL BE THESE MUDDY FOOT-PRINTS...
THEY SUDDENLY DISAPPEAR HALFWAY DOWN.
PI (FLICK)
THIS MUD IS—

G-GROSS!!
WHAT IS THIS SMELLY STUFF!!?
GEHO (CHOKE)
SFX: ZUBO (PLUNGE)
C-COULD THIS BE... HUH? WAIT A MINUTE... THIS IS...
TH-TH-THIS IS... HUH? COULD IT BE?
OH, SHIT!?
NUCHAAA (STIIIICK)
EWWW!!
IT'S SHIT!
NOW THEY'VE DONE IT!
CLEAR MY MIND.
KEEP IT UNDISTURBED.
KYUPON (POP)
I'LL FOLLOW THE TRAIL OF THIS SMELL.
WAY OF THE WOLF'S FANG—
STINKY SMELL SCENT ERASING

I CAN SEE IT!!
BUT FIRST, A SMALL BREAK...
URP!
WELL DONE...
...MINO-MON.
OOK!
NOW... HERE'S A BANANA SNACK AS A REWARD.
SU (SWF)
PAKU (MUNCH)

GASA (RUSTLE)
BANANAS DON'T COUNT AS SNACKS.
BIKUU (JUMP)
EEP!
OOK!?
WH-WH-WHO ARE YOU?
ZA
ZA (ZSH)
SUTA (TMP)
YOU'RE UNDER ARREST.
KUH... IN THAT CASE...
...GO, MINOMON!!
I CHOOSE YOU!
THE SHADY-LOOKING SCHOOLGIRL HAS CHOSEN MINOMON!
BA (BADUM)
OOK EEK EEK—!
!?
KITO!?
BA CHOP
BA
GU (CLENCH)

GOKII (BASH)
EEK!?
OOK...
ACK!
DOSA (WHUD)
PAN (PAT) PAN
EEEEEK!
HM?
ISN'T ...?
... THAT'S ...
ARMBAND: DISCIPLINE
HM ...
WHOA! WHY'RE YOU HERE!?
EEK... PANTIES!!
BA (BLOCK)
SA (SWF)
WEREN'T YOU LOOKING FOR THESE?
S- SORRY.
I'M GOING TO NEED YOU TO HOLD THOSE FOR ME.

FURA (SWAY)
HAAH...
FURA
HAAH...
YOU GOT THE FIRST ONE!!
!!
WELL DONE.
NI (SMILE)
HAAH... HAAH...

MIIIN (BZZZZ)
MIN
MIN
MIIIN
!!
MARO KICHI SAN.
UH... Y-YES?
KURU (TURN)
ARE YOU LISTENING TO ME?
S- SORRY.
YOUR NEXT TARGET...
...IS THE FIERCE FIGHTING EMPRESS MAKOTO.
I WANT YOU...
...TO KEEP AN EYE ON HER.
HUH ...!?
DRAGON 17
SKEWED ACQUAINTANCE

WH-WHY DO I HAVE TO DO THAT!?
W-WAS THAT LAST PERSON...
...EVEN REALLY THAT BAD!?
YO (SOB)
YO
YO
SO YOU DON'T TRUST ME...
...EVEN THOUGH YOU'RE ALL I HAVE, MAROKICHI-SAN...
SHIKU
SHIKU (WEEP)
YOU HAVE NO IDEA HOW BADLY THEY'VE TREATED ME...
O-OKAY. I BELIEVE YOU.
I'M SORRY. I'M SORRY.
B-BUT... CAN WE MAKE THIS THE LAST TIME...
...I EVER HAVE TO DO ANYTHING LIKE THAT AGAIN?

IF THAT PERSON REALLY DID SOME-THING WRONG ...
...THEN WE CAN JUST TALK IT OUT AND ASK HER TO STOP.
とぼ
TOBO
とぼ
TOBO (TRUDGE)
OKAY! ♡ I KNEW I COULD COUNT ON YOU, MAROKICHI-SAN.
NI (GRIND)
I'VE CAUGHT THE CRIMINALS AND RETURNED THE PANTIES.
CASE CLOSED.
YOU WILL RECEIVE COUN-SELING!

SO THESE UNDER-GARMENTS...
...ARE WHAT WERE STOLEN...
SA (SWISH)
GEEH!?
SORRY, BUT COULD YOU DO SOMETHING...
...ABOUT THE WAY YOU'RE HOLDING THOSE? LIKE HIDE THEM...
......
THEN YOU HOLD THEM.
PUI (TURN)
SFX: POI (TOSS)
HUH!?
NO WAY...
WAI...
FUWA (FLOAT)
CLEAR MY MIND.
KEEP IT UNDISTURBED.
SUUUUU (SUUUUUCK)

PUUUUU (PHOOOOOOO)
WAY OF THE CHARGING COW
FUWA (FLOAT)
FUWA
BLOWING PIPE

PUPUUUU (PHOOOO)
FUWA
FUWA
A-ANYWAY, I'D BETTER REPORT TO AYANE-SAN...
NOW YOU'RE DOING PARTY TRICKS...
CHA (CHK)
HUH ...?
A MESSAGE FROM AYANE-SAN...
!!
Can you meet me in the nurse's office?
NURSE'S OFFICE

PASA (POOMF)
HUH...? TH-THESE ARE...
... MINE ...!?

DID SOMETHING HAPPEN?
HAAH!
HAAH!
HAAH!
HAAH!
BLUE IN THE FACE
BIKU (JUMP)
I SHOULD BE ASKING YOU THE SAME THING, MASTER. WHAT HAPPENED...!?
I CAUGHT THE PANTY THIEF.
BA (WHIP)
TH- THANK YOU SO MUCH. JOB WELL DONE!
BUT SOMETHING CAUGHT MY ATTENTION ...
?
ARMBAND: DISCIPLINE
THE FEMALE STUDENT WHO STOL THE UNDER WEAR...
...WAS WEARING AN ARMBAND FROM THE DISCIPLINARY COMMITTEE.
!!
THEN THIS WAS THE WORK OF ITS REMAINING MEMBERS.
DON'T TELL ME...
...THE GUY WHO ATTACKED KEIKO IS ALSO ON THE DISCIPLINARY COMMITTEE, THEN?
HUH ...?
ATTACKED !?

YES...
BY SOME CREATURE THAT LOOKED LIKE A WILD ANIMAL ...
A WILD ANIMAL!?
WHEN I RUSHED OVER...
...HE RAN AWAY.
BUT KEIKO MANAGED TO STEAL THIS OFF OF HIM.
SU (SWF)
HUH...? THIS WATCH...
COULD I SEE IT FOR A SECOND?
SA (SWF)
SURE.
I FEEL LIKE I'VE SEEN THIS SOMEWHERE BEFORE...
OF THE REMAINING DISCIPLINARY COMMITTEE MEMBERS ...
...THERE ARE NONE WHO CAN DEFEAT KEIKO.
SO THIS DOESN'T SEEM RELATED TO THEM ......

YOU SURE ABOUT THAT?
SU (STEP)
!!
AND YOU ARE...?
OH... THIS IS REN-SAN.
SHE'S THE OLDER SISTER OF THAT GIRL WITH THE GLASSES.
THE DRAGON OF SEVERE WAVES ...!?
!!
YOU'RE ...!?
ONE OF THE THREE DRAGONS, DRAGON OF FLASHING STAR AYANE.
AND ONE OF THE EMPRESSES, FIERCE FIGHTING EMPRESS MAKOTO.
I HEARD ABOUT EVERY-THING FROM MELL.
THE LEGEND-ARY DRAGON ...
...IS ON PAR WITH THE HEAVENLY RULING TIGER ...!!
JIRI (SCUFF)

PIRI (TENSE)
HEH...
NO NEED FOR THAT.
I DIDN'T COME HERE FOR YOU.
MAS-TER...
...DO YOU KNOW HER?
WE JUST MET.
NOW IF YOU WOULD PLEASE SHUT YOUR MOUTHS—
YOUR RIGHT-HAND WOMAN WAS TARGETED, DRAGON OF FLASHING STAR.
AND BY STEALING YOUR PANTIES, YOU WERE LEFT PARALYZED.
ATTACKS
CAN'T MOVE
FINDS
IT'S SAFE TO ASSUME THAT THEY'RE SEEKING TO DIVIDE YOUR FORCES.

THEN THEIR NEXT TARGET ...
...IS ME...?
!?
MAKOTO ...?
KEIKO WAS TAKEN BY SURPRISE.
SHE WAS SERIOUSLY INJURED... SO...
...I WILL GO CONFRONT THEM.
HUH!?
I WILL ACT AS A DECOY...
ZA (ZSH)
...TO LURE OUT THE PERPETRATOR.
AYANE... I'M SORRY, BUT I'LL NEED YOUR BACKING—
NO!

I'LL BE THE DECOY!!
SU (STEP)
WHAT!?
THE REASON KEIKO AND YOU ARE BEING TARGETED ...
...IS PROBABLY TO ISOLATE ME...
I'M THEIR FINAL TARGET...
THERE'S NO NEED FOR YOU TO PUT YOURSELF IN HARM'S WAY, MAKOTO.
BUT AYANE—
YOU UNDERSTAND THE DANGER YOU'RE IN, DON'T YOU?
......
I DON'T CARE WHAT HAPPENS TO ME.
BUT...

...I WON'T FORGIVE ANYONE...
...WHO HURTS MY FRIENDS.
......
HMPH... SO YOU'RE THAT TYPE.
GEEZ... ONCE YOU PUT YOUR MIND TO SOMETHING, YOU DON'T BACK DOWN.
I'LL COVER YOU.
THANKS, MAKOTO.
UH... I'LL HELP TOO.
DA (DASH)
......
TA (TMP)

KEIKO WAS ATTACKED BEHIND THE GYM.
LET'S GO SOMEWHERE OUT OF THE WAY.
TA
TA
TA (TMP)
MM-HM!!
WHERE ARE THEY GOING?
MAROKICHI-KUN!?
FURA
!!
FURA (SWAY)
FURA
RINTARO-SAN...
!!
SU (STEP)
WH-WHAT'S WRONG?
WEREN'T YOU GOING HOME?
FURA
UH... NO... WELL...

YOU'RE BARELY WALKING STRAIGHT. ARE YOU SURE YOU'RE OKAY!?
FURA
ガシ
GASHI (GRAB)
UH... SORRY.
!?
YOU'RE BURNING UP. WE'VE GOTTA GET YOU TO THE NURSE.
I...I'M FINE...
HAAH!
HAAH!
YOU ARE NOT OKAY!
NURSE'S OFFICE
ALMOST THERE...
JUST A LITTLE FURTHER ...
?
SORRY...
!!

SA (SSK)
Y-YOU OKAY? MAYBE YOU HAVE HEAT STROKE ...
WANT SOMETHING TO DRINK?
OR SHOULD WE FAN YOU?
S-SORRY, BUT I'M REALLY OKAY...
AIR CONDITIONER, CHECK.
TEKI
PAKI (HUSTLE)
TEKI PAKI (BUSTLE)
CURTAINS, CHECK.
DEHUMIDIFIER, CHECK.
Y-YOU DON'T HAVE TO DO ALL THIS FOR ME...

U-UM..
WHY ARE YOU BEING SO NICE TO ME, RINTARO-SAN?
WE BARELY KNOW EACH OTHER...
!!
HUH ...?

I'M REALLY GLAD WE MET.

FOR A GUY LIKE ME WHO CAN'T HANDLE GIRLS...

...THE ONES AT NANGOKUREN ARE WAY TOO UNDER-DRESSED.

IT'S REALLY HARD...

Y-YOU'RE RIGHT. THEY'RE DEFINITELY TOO EXPOSED.

THE ROAD TO NORMALCY ...
...IS A DREAM WITHIN A DREAM.
EVEN IF WE COULD BECOME NORMAL...
...I HAVE A FEELING IT'D BRING US EVEN MORE MISFORTUNE.
HA! HA! HA! HA!
......
YOU REALLY ARE A GOOD GUY, RINTARO-SAN.
BUT I'M...
I'M ACTUALLY KIND OF WORTHLESS ...
HUH ...?

I'VE NEVER BEEN SOMEONE PEOPLE COULD RELY ON.
AND I CAN'T SAY NO WHEN PEOPLE ASK ME TO DO THINGS...
SO WHAT!?
!!
UNTIL I CAME TO NAN-GOKUREN...
...ACTUALLY, IT MIGHT STILL HOLD TRUE EVEN NOW...
...I'D LIVED MY WHOLE LIFE ALWAYS JUST THINKING ABOUT MYSELF.
YOU, ON THE OTHER HAND...
...DO THINGS TO HELP OTHERS, YOU KNOW?

AND THAT'S AS UPSTANDING AS IT GETS.
TH-THANK...
...YOU...
RIN-TARO-SAN...
KYU (SQUINT)
U-UM...
THE TRUTH IS, I—
BIII (BEEP)
BIII
BIII
!!
OH, THAT REMINDS ME...
ZUBO (DIG)

I NEVER GAVE THIS BACK TO AYANE-SAN...
SU (FWIP)
!!
DOKI (BADUM)
HM...?
AYANE-SAN...?
......
AH!!
AYANE-SAN!!
U-UU-UH...
WHERE DID SHE GO?
PER-HAPS...
SU (POINT)
TH-THAT WAY!?
THANKS!
MARO-KICHI-KUN, SORRY.
KURU (TURN)

I'VE GOTTA GO...
BASA (FWAP)
HUH?
MAROKICHI-KUN...?
A-ANYWAY, I'VE GOTTA GO...!
TA (TMP)
TA
REPORT-ING IN.
THE TEAM RESPONSIBLE FOR THE UN-DERGARMENT THEFTS HAS BEEN APPRE-HENDED.
HUH, IS THAT SO...
WELL, AT LEAST THE HARDY SWALLOW IS DOWN FOR THE COUNT.

THERE'S MORE—
THE DRAGON OF FLASHING STAR IS CURRENTLY ACTING ON HER OWN.
PIKU (PERK)
AND MARO-KICHI?
WELL...
HE HASN'T BEEN SIGHTED FOR A WHILE NOW.
ALTHOUGH HE'S BEEN SUMMONED...
TCH... THAT LOSER.
THIS KIND OF OPPOR-TUNITY DOESN'T COME TWICE.
GIRI (GRIT)
RUMINA-SAN...
...UNTIL MAROKICHI ARRIVES...
...I'M GOING TO STALL HER.
ZA (ZSH)
YES, MA'AM!!

チラ
CHIRA (GLANCE)
SFX: PIKU (PERK)
ピク
GYU
GYU (WHOOSH)

DOGO (BASH)
BA (HOP)
!?
GYUN (ZOOM)
SUTA (TAP)
TA (TMP)
KUH...
!!
GASHI (GRAB)
JARI (JANGLE)

IT SEEMS YOU'VE IMPROVED...
... ASUNA!!
JARI
HEH HEH...
I'M NOT THE ONLY ONE...
...WHO HASN'T WASTED HER TIME IN IDLENESS.
ZA (ZSH)
!!
EVER SINCE YOU DISASSEM-BLED THE DISCIPLINARY COMMITTEE ...
...ALL I'VE THOUGHT ABOUT IS HOW TO DEFEAT YOU.

HASU
HASU
HASU
HASU (PANT)
I'M GOING TO TAKE YOUR DRAGON NAME...
...AND REGAIN THE DRAGON OF STORMING JADE'S RESPECT ONCE MORE! ♥
MY COM-RADES' PAIN...
GU (GRIP)
...IS MINE AS WELL.
BAKII (SHATTER)
YOUR WISH...
...WILL BE SHATTERED ALONG WITH YOUR DREAMS.
HEH HEH ...
ENOUGH JOKING.
POI (TOSS)

SORRY I'M LATE.
... ASUNA-SAN.
TA
TA
TA (TMP)
!!
MARO-KICHI-SAAAN! ♥
?
TA
THANK GOODNES YOU'RE HERE. ♥
MUGYU (MOOSH)
NOW BEAT UP THIS GIRL. ♥
MMPH!
PYON (POUNCE)
GU
GU (SHOVE)
P-PLEASE STOP THAT...
!?
MARO-KICHI-SAN?

I THINK WHAT YOU'RE DOING...
...IS WRONG, ASUNA-SAN...
......
YOU'RE SO MEAN, MAROKICHI-SAN!
I THOUGHT YOU WERE ON MY SIDE!
UH...
I THOUGHT YOU WERE THE ONLY ONE...
...WHO UNDERSTOOD HOW I FELT...
TH-THAT'S ...
IF YOU HATE ME NOW...
...THEN JUST SAY IT TO MY FACE...
PORO (DRIP)
—!!
THIS REALLY IS...
...THE LAST TIME.

THANKS. ♥
I'M SO HAPPY...
!!
PAFU (POOMF)
HM. ♥
HAH! ♥
PAFU
PAFU
PAFU
PAFU
MMMPH!
!?
WH- WHAT ARE YOU DOING!?
UUH... GGHH...
FURA (SWAY)
B- BOO...
BOO...
GU
GU (STRAIN)
GISHI (RIP)
BOGO (BULGE)
BIGI (TEAR)

KA (FLASH)
ZUUUN (THOOOOM)
BOOOOBIIIIIIES!
!?
ZA (ZSH)
WE WIN...
REN-SAN, ARE YOU SURE IT WAS THIS WAY!?
MAYBE THAT WAY.
OH MY GOD !!

DRAGON 18 BEST FRIENDS

GUN (LUNGE)
BA
BA (HOP)
GOGA (BASH)
BA
BA
TAN (TMP)
BA
TAN

BA
BA
GUH!
GA
KUH!
GA
(BAM)
TAN
GUH...

!?
GYUN
(ZOOM)
DOGA
(SMASH)
UGUH!
GUH...
GAKU
(DROP)
HAH...
BYO
(WHOOSH)

GO (BASH)
MAKO-TO!!
ARE YOU OKAY!?
GA (GRAB)
......
KOKI KOKI (CRACK)
TON TON (TMP)
!!

DOGYU (ZOOM)
!!
I CAN'T EVEN FOLLOW HER...
REMINDS ME OF YAMCHA.
JI (STARE)
BOPA (BULGE)
BACHUN (ZANG)

HUH!?
UGH...
GOGA (WHACK)
KUH...
KURU (SPIN)
!?
HYU (SWOOSH)

GOKI (CRACK)
GYUOOO (WHOOSH)
!?
MAS-TER!!
TA (TMP)
DOGOO (BOOM)

SORRY I'M LATE.
I CAN'T TELL HER I GOT LOST...
PYON (HOP)
KITO AND I WILL LOOK AFTER THE FIERCE FIGHTING EMPRESS.
TH- THANK YOU!
RINTARO AGAIN.
HE'S SO WILY.
GIRI (GRINT)
MARO-KICHI-SAN.
FINISH THEM.
PARA (FLAKE)
SHIIIIN (SILENCE)
PARA
HUH ...?
MARO-KICHI-SAN...?

DOGYA (CRASH)
!!
BUN (SWING)
GA (BAM)
GOSHI (SMASH)

GA
GA
(CRUNCH)
GA
GA
BUN
(FLING)
BON
(BULGE)
BACHUN
(ZIP)

GYUDO
(ZWAM)
GOGA
(CRASH)
M-
MAS-
TER...
HOOO
HO
HO
HO!
WHAT
FUN!
WHAT
PLEA-
SURE!

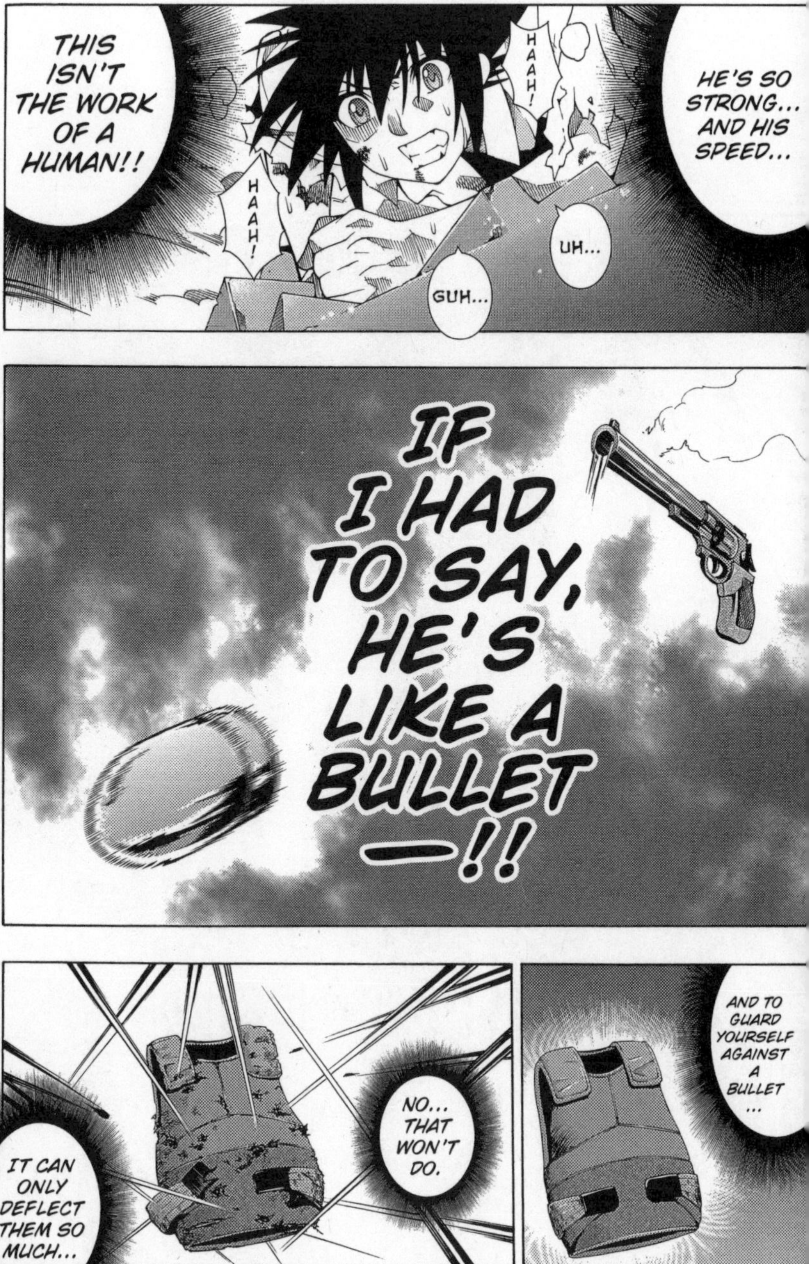

IF I HAD TO SAY, HE'S LIKE A BULLET—!!

M-MASTER!
I'LL HELP TOO!
GU GU (STRAIN)
N-NO, I'M FINE...
B-BUT...!!
A WEAPON SUPERIOR TO A BULLET...
HUH...?
PHOO...
HAAH...
PHOO...
HAAH...
FUO (WHOOSH)

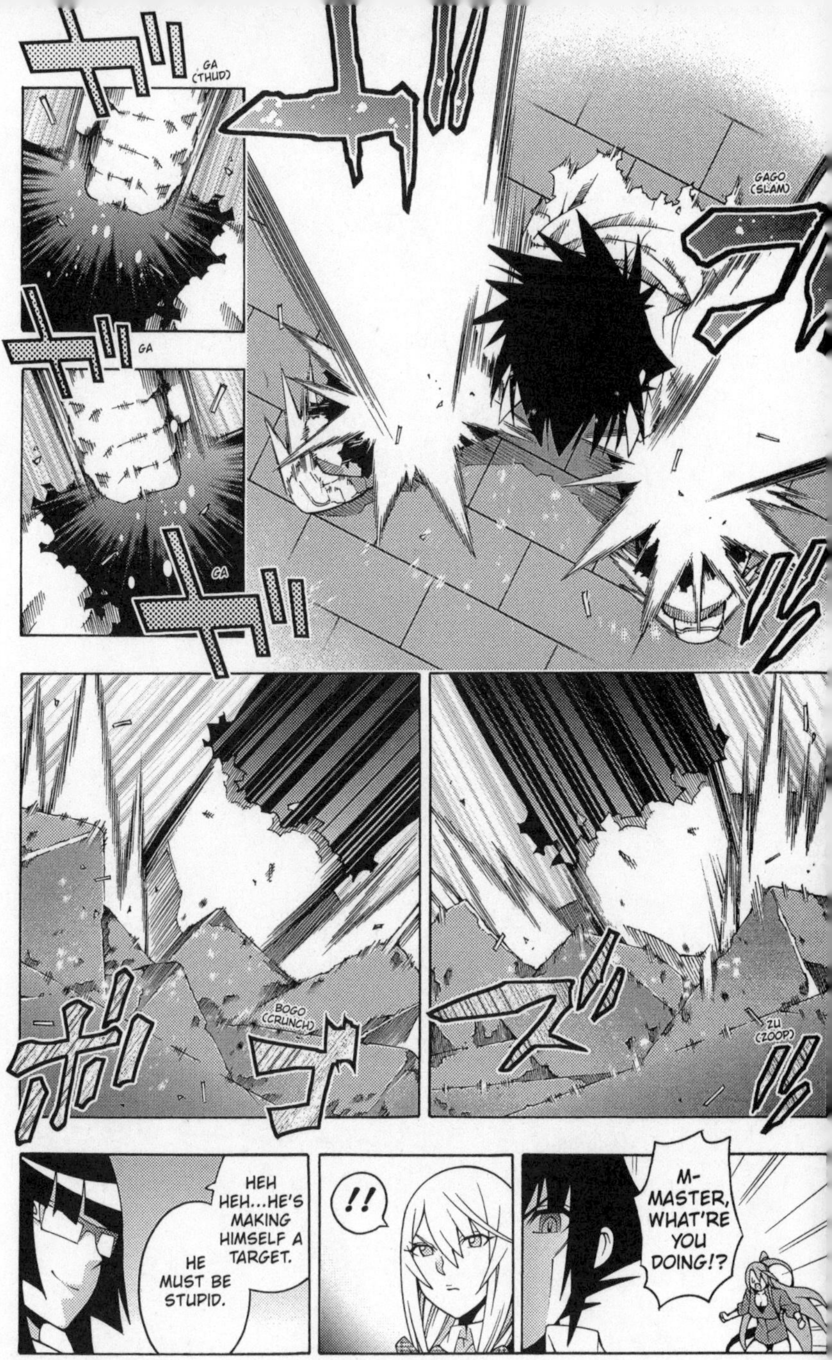

GAGO
(SLAM)
GA
(THUD)
GA
GA
ZU
(ZOOP)
BOGO
(CRUNCH)
M-MASTER, WHAT'RE YOU DOING!?
!!
HEH HEH...HE'S MAKING HIMSELF A TARGET.
HE MUST BE STUPID.

FUOOOOO (WOOOO)
SU (BREATHE)
CLEAR MY MIND.
PHOOO ...
KEEP IT UNDIS-TURBED.
GISHI (BULGE)
BON (BOOSH)
BACHUN (ZOOM)
MAS-TER—
...

WAY OF THE CHARGING COW—
BULLET CUTTING HORNS
SUU (SWF)
GYUN (ZOOM)

BACHIIIII
(SMAAASH)
!?
WHA ...!?
GA
(THUD)
BOO
(BAM)
DOGO
(CRASH)

WH-WHAT ON EARTH...?
HERE'S SOME TRIVIA FOR YOU.
HUH?
WHEN YOU PIT A STATIONARY BUTTER KNIFE AGAINST A BULLET...
...THE BULLET WILL ACTUALLY GET CLEAVED IN HALF.
IN THIS CASE, WITH HIS HIGH POWER AND SPEED...

FURA (SWAY)
FURA
GU-GEH...
UGH...
...THE DAMAGE CAME BACK AT HIM INSTEAD.
PARA (FLAKE)
PARA
GARA (CRMBL)
GARA
THAT'S WHAT RINTARO WAS AIMING FOR.
WOW... YOU'RE RIGHT.
...
ZUBO (POP)
SHURU (SHRINK)
RU
RU
RU
HAAH...
HAAH...

MARO... KICHI...
...KUN...?
AH!!
I'M SORRY, RINTARO-SAN.
I'M REALLY SORRY.
GO (BASH)
W- WAIT A SECOND.
MARO-KICHI-KUN... WHY!?
WH- WHAT'S GOING ON HERE!?
......
GYU (PURSE)

JOINT INVOLUNTARY EMBARRASS-MENT PERVERSION SYNDROME.
CALLED "BEEFY DUDE SYNDROME" FOR SHORT.
WHEN I GET AROUSED...
...MY MUSCLES UNDERGO AN UNNATURAL PROCESS OF ENLARGEMENT.
I LOSE MY SENSE OF SELF AND GO ON A RAMPAGE...
WHEN THAT HAPPENS ...
...THERE'S NO TELLING WHAT I MIGHT DO...
I'VE HURT YOU...
I WAS WRONG TO LISTEN TO HER!!
......

ZA (ZSH)
ZA
ZA
ZA
PITA (PAUSE)
!!
SU (SWF)
BIKU (JUMP)
......

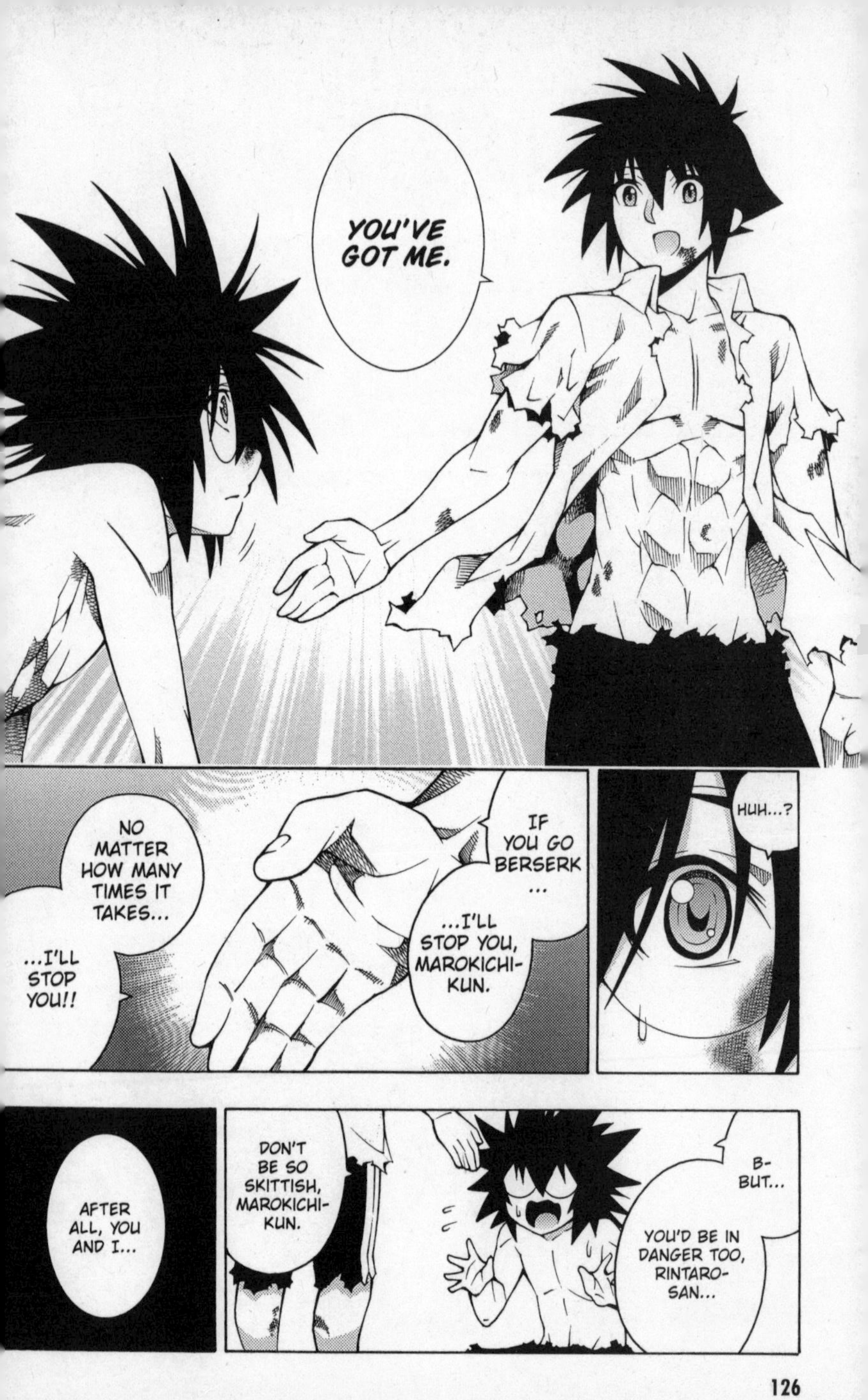
YOU'VE GOT ME.
HUH...?
IF YOU GO BERSERK...
...I'LL STOP YOU, MAROKICHI-KUN.
NO MATTER HOW MANY TIMES IT TAKES...
...I'LL STOP YOU!!
B-BUT...
YOU'D BE IN DANGER TOO, RINTARO-SAN...
DON'T BE SO SKITTISH, MAROKICHI-KUN.
AFTER ALL, YOU AND I...

...ARE COMRADE IN BEING SHY AROUND GIRLS.
NIKO (GRIN)
WE'RE FRIENDS.
RIN-TARO-SAN...
ALL RIGHT!
GA (GRAB)
GU
GU (CLENCH)

HOW DARE YOU...
DOTE (SPLAT)
YIKES!
...SETTLE YOUR DIFFERENCES LIKE THIS!?
BUN (SWING)
WAH!
SA (SCOOT)
I DON'T WANT TO SEE GUYS BEING AFFECTIONATE!
ARE YOU TRYING TO WIN THE ATTENTION OF FUJOSHI!?
KA (FLASH)
ARE YOU GONNA XXX AND XXX!?
HUH!?
ZA (ZSH)
WAH!
WAH!
BASA (FLAP)
GIVE 'EM A FEEL!!
PURU (JIGGLE)
NYA-HEE!

I DO CARE
...ABOUT YOUR CONDITION.
JUST BEAT DOWN THAT DRAGON OF FLASHING STAR.
YOU LOSER!
MONYUN (MOOSH
N- NO!
STOP IT!!
KN- KNOCK IT OFF!
FEELING REAL BOOBS FOR THE FIRST TIME IS AMAZING, ISN'T IT?
SU (SIT)
UUH...
GHRK...
BAIN (BOING)
EEK!
BIKUN (JOLT)
R...
R...
R- R...
REAL...
...BOO- BIES...
BON (BULGE)

ZUUUN (THOOM)
FIRST REAL FEEL!
!?
HE'S EVEN BIGGER THAN BEFORE ...!!
THAT'S THE STUFF, MAROKICHI. ♡
KUNE (WRIGGLE)
KUNE
GET EVEN BIGGER AND BIGGER.
KUH...
N-NOT AGAIN...
GGH...
NGH...
NAAH ...

SHURU (SHRINK)
RU
RU
RU
!!
HUH ...?
WH-WHAT HAP-PENED!?
WHY'S HE REVERTING BACK TO NORMAL!?
SHUUUU (SSSHH)
KO (CLACK)

SHUUUUU (SSSSHHH)
HE SHRANK...
IS THAT THE PINK MAJIN...? HIS BATTLE POWER IS 530,000...
DON'T SAY THAT OUT LOUD ...!!

DRAGON 19 A BOLT FROM THE BLUE

ZA (ZSH)
!?
HUH...!
WAIT A MIN-UTE!?
PURIN (JIGGLE)
JIII (STARE)
NIYA (GRIN)
BA (BAH)
TH- THAT'S IT, MAROKICHI!!
THAT'S SOME SPEED...
NOW HURRY UP AND FINISH HER OFF!!
U-WHOA!?
JIRO (GLARE)

すぽん
SUPON (BARE)
ニャニャ
NIYA
NIYA
WH-WHAT ARE YOU DOING TO ME, YOU JERK!!
!!
ニッ
NI (GRIN)
FU (FZZT)

BA (FWIP)
!?
ZUZA (SKID)
ZA
NO.
MARO-KICHI-KUN.
IRA (RIK)
THIS ISN'T WHAT YOU WANT.
GO BACK TO NORMAL ...!!

HYUBI (SWISH)
!?
GA (WHACK)
GUH!
GYUDO (ZWAM)
GU-HAH!
ZA (SKID)
ZA
ZA
HIS POWER AND SPEED ARE JUST THE SAME...
...BUT THE PRECISION OF HIS ATTACKS IS ON A WHOLE NEW LEVEL...!!
KOFF!
KOFF!

!!
ZA (ZISH)
HYU (WHOOSH)
KUH...
BA (BLOCK)
GU-HAH!
BACHIIN (CRACK)

ZUZA (ZSSH)
UH... GUH...
I CAN'T TOTALLY BLOCK HIM...!!
HAAH!
AND I DON'T THINK I CAN DODGE HIM EITHER...
HAAH!
IF I CAN'T GUARD OR EVADE...
...THEN —
YURA (WAVER)
HYU (WHOOSH)
CLEAR MY MIND.
KEEP IT UNDIS-TURBED.
HYU

WAY OF THE SPARROW'S WING—
WHITE STEEL WORLD
GA
GA
GA (WHACK)
GA
GA
GA
...I'LL ALWAYS MAKE THE FIRST MOVE!!
I CAN'T BELIEVE THE MASTER'S ATTACKING SO MUCH...
I'VE NEVER SEEN THIS BEFORE...
IT'S NOT WORKING THOUGH. EVERY PUNCH IS BEING COUNTERED.
WH-WHAT'S GOING ON? THOSE TWO ARE...
I CAN'T EVEN FOLLOW THEM ANYMORE.

GO
(BASH)
BIRI
BIRI
BIRI
(STING)
KUH
KUH...
GU-
HAH!
KUH
KAH!
GA
(WHAM)
KUH...
BIRI
BIRI
BIRI
THIS
HURTS
LIKE
HELL...
BUT...
...FOR
SOME
REA-
SON...

...IT'S FUN!!
UP TILL NOW, I HAVEN'T BEEN ABLE TO FOCUS WHEN I FIGHT.
BUT NOW...
...NOTHING'S HOLDING ME BACK. I CAN PULL OUT ALL THE STOPS.
I'VE NEVER FELT THIS WAY BEFORE...
I NEVER KNEW THAT FIGHTING COULD BE THIS MUCH FUN...
DON (SLAM)
GAH...

ZUZA (SKID)
ZA
......
JIRI (SCUFF)
GUI (WIPE)
ぐいっ
YOU'RE STRONG.
HAAH ...
THE NEXT ATTACK WILL PROBABLY BE THE LAST...
I'M GOING TO SHOW YOU...
...HOW I'VE SURPASSED MYSELF.

HYU (WHOOSH)
GUH...
GYAGO (ZWANG)
THE SCHOOL...
SUU (SWFF)
...OF THE BLUE MOON REFLECTED ON A LAKE
TA
TA (TMP)
KURU (SPIN)

WAY OF THE WOLF'S FANG—
ZAKII (SLICE)
ROCK CRUSHING BULLET KICK
ZUGO (ZOOM)
JI (STARE)
KO (CRACK)

BOGOO (CRUNCH)
KAH KAH!
BA (WHIP)
!!
THE SCHOOL...
...OF THE BLUE MOON REFLECTED ON A LAKE

A FEINT!?
HE CAUGHT HIM OFF GUARD...
GIRYU (SQUEAK)
KUH...
GU (BULGE)
BIKI (ZING)
TON (TAP)
WAY OF THE LUNGING BOAR —

SOLID STEEL SLICE
DO (SLAM)
DOSA (SPLAT)

HAAAH!
HAAAH!
DO
I D-DID IT...TWO SCHOOL OF THE BLUE MOON REFLECTED ON A LAKE MOVES IN A ROW.
HAAH!
HAAH!
THAT OUGHT TO DO IT...
QUICK SUCCESSION OF TWO TECHNIQUES THAT USE MASSIVE AMOUNTS OF POWER.
THAT'D BE IMPOSSIBLE IF NOT FOR A TOUGH BODY AND IRON-STRONG WILL...
IM-PRES-SIVE!!
MAS-TER!!
TA (TMP)

GABA (RISE)
SHIT! IT'S STILL NO GOOD!?
GRR...
GRK...
UGEEEEEH!
BUN (SHAKE)
BUN
BUN
GUGAAAAH!
DO (SLAM)
ZA (ZSH)
ZA
BA (LUNGE)

GYUN (ZOOM)
!?
EE...
DO (THUD)
GU
GU (STRAIN)
NO!! MARO-KICHI-KUN!!
PHOOO ...
SUU (SWF)
!?
TH-THIS FEELING...

STILL YOUR HEART...
...LIKE THE BLUE MOON REFLECTED ON A LAKE.
CLEAR MY MIND.
KEEP IT UNDIS-TURBED...
URRAAAH!
THIS...
BA (LEAP)
THE SCHOOL OF THE BLUE MOON REFLECTED ON A LAKE
KA (FLASH)
GAKIN (SHING)
WAY OF THE TIGER'S JAW—

BOULDER SHATTERING ROAR OF RUIN

ZUGO (LUNGE)
DOBACHI (SMACK)
SHUUUU (SSSSHHH)
FU (PHEW)

GAKUN (DROP)
HAAH!
HAAH!
SFX: HOGEEE (STUNNED)
TH-THAT WAS THE SCHOOL OF THE BLUE MOON RE-FLECTED ON A LAKE JUST NOW!!
H-HOW DID YOU LEARN IT SO QUICKLY!?
ほげ〜
HOW MANY HOURS, MINUTES, AND SECONDS DID IT TAKE!? HOW MANY REVOLUTIONS OF THE EARTH!?
EVER SINCE WE FIRST MET...
...I'VE BEEN WATCHING YOU MORE CLOSELY THAN ANYBODY.
THE SPECIAL TRAINING YOU GAVE ME...
...I HAVE KEPT UP EVERY SINGLE DAY!!

UH... OH... THAT.
N- N-NOW I SEE!!
SPECIAL TRAINING...? EXERCISES ...?
THAT REMINDS ME, I ALMOST FORGOT THAT HAPPENED.
HAAH.
BUT I STILL LACK THE STAMINA FOR IT.
HAAH.
I CAN'T BELIEVE JUST ONE TECHNIQUE USES THIS MUCH STRENGTH.
UH...
SA (SWISH)
D-DON'T WORRY, YOU DID A GREAT JOB ANYWAY.
NOW MARO-KICHI-KUN IS...
MARO-KICHI-KUN!?
SHIIIIN (SILENCE)
HUP!
GOGA (BASH)

SFX: FURA (WOBBLE) FURA

GU-GGH...
GG-HH...
HA-AH!
HA-AH!
GARA (CRMBL)
GARA
PARA (FLAKE)
PARA
!!
H-HE'S STILL NOT BACK TO NORMAL ...!?
GH...
GRR...
!?
BIKU (JUMP)
NNGH...
E... EE...
KUNE (TWIST)
KUNE
EE... EEE-EEE...
UNE (WRIGGLE)
UNE
HAAH!
EEE... EE...
UUH...
EE...
GUH...
HAAH!
SHUUUU (SSSHHH)
WE DID IT!
I DON'T KNOW HOW, BUT...
...MARO-KICHI-KUN'S BACK TO NORMAL, GUYS!!
BA (WHIP)

PITA
(PAUSE)
DANGER
PERON
(DANGLE)
SHUBA
(SWF)
しゅばっ
AN EEL.
GROSS.
SFX: SA (SPURN)
KURA
(JOLT)
HUH...?
EEL?
EEEL!?
GEEEEEH!

N-NO, THIS ISN'T AN EEL.
IT'S NOT AN EEL!!
BA (FWIP)
GYU (TUG)
<THIS IS...>
<...NOT AN EEL!>
IT'S NOT AN EEL, AND IF I HAD TO SAY...
...I'LL HAVE TO GO CHECK WITH YAHOO ANSWERS.
FURU
SCARY.
FURU (TRMBL)
SO HIS SEXUAL AROUSAL WAS QUELLED BY THE EEL...
IT MUST HAVE CAUSED SOME CONSIDERABLE DAMAGE TO HIS PSYCHE...
URF!
RINTARO, IF HE EVER LOSES CONTROL AGAIN, JUST SHOW IT TO MAKE HIM STOP.
YOUR LITTLE... EE... EEEE...
URF!
ONE LITTLE EEL, AND THE WHOLE PROBLEM'S PUT TO REST!!
NO WAY!
SHUT UP WITH THE EEL TALK!
RINTARO-SAN, THANK YOU SO MUCH.
AS A PREVENTATIVE MEASURE, I'D LIKE A SHOT OF YOUR EEL FOR MY CELL PHONE BACKGROUND.
UH, I THINK THAT'S GETTING INTO ILLEGAL TERRITORY.

SFX: WACHA (CLAMOR) WACHA

SU (STAND)
......
TOBO TOBO (TRUDGE)
ASUNA-SAN!!
PLEASE LET ME KNOW IF YOU EVER NEED HELP.
FOR OTHER MATTERS, I MEAN...
I MAY NOT BE MUCH USE, BUT...
...I THINK I CAN HELP YOU.
......
YOU'LL FORGET ABOUT ME SOON ANYWAY...

I'LL BE WAITING FOR YOU.
ALWAYS ...
!!
DOKI (BADUM)
WH-WHAT'S THAT SUP-POSED TO MEAN!?
YOU CAN WAIT THE REST OF YOUR LIFE, FOR ALL I CARE!
WE'RE LEAVING, RUMINA-SAN.
YES, MA'AM.
SUTA (MARCH)
SUTA SUTA SUTA
PEKO (BOW)
HIIIIN (VWEEEEE)
!?
GOO (WHOOSH)
GARA (RATTLE)

BA (HOP)
HUH... MELL-SAN!?
!!
BAHO (POOF)
I'M HERE —
REN!
TA (TMP)
BI (JAB)

......
...WHY?
GYAAAAAH!
SO THAT YOU AND RIN-CHAN CAN GET ALONG!
YOU DON'T HAVE TO WORRY ABOUT THAT ANYMORE, MELL.
HUH?
I'VE ALREADY MADE UP MY MIND...
?
...ABOUT RINTARO.
THE REASON I CAME TO THIS SCHOOL...
...WAS TO MAKE SURE THAT YOU...
...COULD INHERIT THE PLEDGE OF HEAVENLY WAVES.
BUT I SEE NOW THAT IT WAS NEEDLESS TO WORRY...
O... OKAY.
PYON (HOP)
TOLD YOU SO.
HM!

I'M COUNTING ON YOU...
...TO LOOK AFTER MY LITTLE SISTER RINO...
... RINTARO.
I'LL D-DO WHAT I CAN...
BUT!!
DON'T YOU DARE THINK OF TAKING HER HAND IN MARRIAGE.
GIRO (GLARE)
RIGHT!! THAT'S NOT AN ISSUE.
HEH...
JIIII (STARE)
?
UH... EXCUSE ME...
WH-WHAT IS IT?
WHAT'S THIS!?

TO BE CONTINUED

DRAGONS RIOTING 4

TSUYOSHI WATANABE

Translation: Christine Dashiell

Lettering: Anthony Quintessenza

Yen Press
1290 Avenue of the Americas
New York, NY 10104

Library of Congress Control Number: 2015952605

ISBNs: 978-0-316-30880-9 (paperback)
978-0-316-30885-4 (ebook)
978-0-316-27618-4 (app)

10 9 8 7 6 5 4 3 2 1

BVG

Printed in the United States of America